THE BODHISATTVA ASSUMED MANY FORMS THROUGH MANY LIFE CYCLES. AND SO IT WAS THAT WHEN BRAHMADATTA REIGNED IN VARANASI, HE WAS BORN AN ELEPHANT IN A FOREST IN THE HIMALAYAS.

* BASED ON SEELAVA NAGARAJA JATAKA

THE ELEPHANT GREW UP IN THE FOREST, WITH OTHER LITTLE ELEPHANTS.
LET'S SHAKE THIS BRANCH TO FRIGHTEN THE MONKEY ON IT.
WATCH ME SUCK THIS SQUIRREL INTO MY TRUNK.

AS HE GREW OLDER, HE NOTICED THAT MOST OF HIS COMPANIONS WERE SELFISH, GREEDY, EVEN CRUEL.
AAAH! AAAH!

THE WHITE ELEPHANT DECIDED TO LEAVE THE HERD.
I DON'T BELONG HERE. I'D RATHER LIVE ALONE.

AND SO HE DWELT APART, GIVING HELP AND GOOD COUNSEL WHEN NEEDED. ONE DAY HE SAW A LITTLE MONKEY WEEPING.
WHY ARE YOU CRYING?
I'M SMALL AND WEAK. MY FRIENDS TEASE ME.

HE GOT THE THOUGHTLESS MONKEYS TOGETHER.
SHAME ON YOU! WHY DO YOU HARASS YOUR WEAKER BROTHER, YOU WHO SHOULD PROTECT HIM? HAVE YOU NOT HEARD THE STORY OF...?
MANY AN EVENING FOUND HIM ADVISING AN EAGER GROUP OF ANIMALS, YOUNG AND OLD. SOON HE CAME TO BE KNOWN AS GOOD KING ELEPHANT.

ONE DAY, A FORESTER FROM VARANASI LOST HIS WAY IN THAT FOREST.
I HAVE NEVER FELT MORE FRIGHTENED IN MY LIFE. EVERY PATH SEEMS TO LEAD ME FARTHER AWAY FROM HOME.

AS THE LIGHT GREW FAINTER —
EEOW! WHAT WAS THAT?
OH! IT WAS ONLY A SHADOW HOW FOOLISH OF ME!
GATHERING COURAGE, HE WALKED ON. SUDDENLY —
AN ELEPHANT! I'M AS GOOD AS DEAD!
HEAVEN HELP ME! I'LL BE CRUSHED TO PULP!

WHY, HE SEEMS HARMLESS! HE'S ONLY FOLLOW-ING ME, NOT CHASING ME AS I THOUGHT.
EVERY TIME HE MOVED, THE ELEPHANT FOLLOWED. EVERY TIME HE STOPPED THE ELEPHANT TOO STOPPED.
I'LL TURN ROUND AND STOP. LET'S SEE WHAT HE DOES.
TO HIS SURPRISE, THE ANIMAL SPOKE TO HIM
I HEARD YOU SCREAM. IS THERE ANYTHING I CAN DO FOR YOU?
WHAT A KIND, GENTLE VOICE! AND YET, SO DEEP AND POWERFUL!
I'VE LOST MY WAY. I WANT TO GO TO VARANASI.
COME HOME WITH ME. I'LL GUIDE YOU TO THE CITY.

LATER, AT THE ELEPHANT'S CAVE —
YOU ARE EXHAUSTED. WHY DON'T YOU REST HERE FOR A FEW DAYS?
I THINK I WILL.
THE ELEPHANT'S DAY BEGAN EARLY.
I LIKE TO WATCH THE DAY BREAK OVER THOSE HILLS AS I BATHE.
IN THE EVENING THEY WALKED TO A CLEARING IN THE FOREST.
LET US WATCH THE SUN GO DOWN. IT FILLS MY HEART WITH PEACE.
I ENVY YOU, YOUR PEACE OF MIND. WE MEN ARE RESTLESS CREATURES.

AFTER A FEW DAYS—
I'D LOVE TO STAY ON, BUT I HAVE WORK TO DO IN VARANASI.
I'LL TAKE YOU TO THE EDGE OF THE FOREST AND SET YOU ON YOUR WAY TO THE CITY.
I MUST REMEMBER THIS CLUMP OF TREES...
...AND THIS HILL AND THIS WINDING PATH.
I MAY NEED TO COME BACK SOME DAY.

AT THE EDGE OF THE FOREST, HE DISMOUNTED.
THERE LIES THE ROAD TO VARANASI.
THANK YOU, MY FRIEND.
AND REMEMBER, YOU MUST KEEP MY HAUNTS A SECRET FROM ALL MEN.
A FEW DAYS LATER, THE FORESTER HAPPENED TO VISIT THE IVORY BAZAAR AT VARANASI.
WHAT BEAUTIFUL THINGS YOU CREATE!
THEY COULD BE EVEN MORE BEAU-TIFUL, BUT GOOD TUSKS ARE HARD TO COME BY.
ARE THEY? WOULD THE TUSK OF A LIVING ELEPHANT BE GOOD ENOUGH?
IT'S THE BEST. BUT IT'S RARE AND COSTS MUCH MORE THAN THE TUSK OF A DEAD ONE.
GREED GOT THE BETTER OF THE FORESTER. HE WENT BACK TO THE FOREST.
WHAT IS THE MATTER? YOU LOOK UNHAPPY.
I AM UP TO MY NECK IN DEBT. A PIECE OF YOUR TUSK. CAN SAVE ME.

THE ELEPHANT SAT DOWN AND HELD HIS TRUNK OUT OBLIGINGLY.
I WILL GLADLY GIVE YOU BOTH MY TUSKS. BUT YOU WILL HAVE TO CUT THEM OFF.
I CAME PREPARED. I KNEW YOU WOULD NOT FAIL ME.
WHAT YOU HOLD ARE NO ORDINARY TUSKS. THEY ARE THE SOURCE OF ALL MY WISDOM.
BACK IN VARANASI, THE FORESTER RECEIVED A BIG SUM OF MONEY FOR THE TUSKS.
WHY, THERE IS MORE MONEY IN THIS THAN I THOUGHT! NOW I CAN BUY ALL THE SILKS AND JEWELS I WANT.
A MONTH LATER—
AFTER I BUY THESE THERE'LL BE NO MONEY LEFT. I SHOULD HAVE CUT CLOSER TO THE FLESH. WHAT A WASTE OF GOOD IVORY.

THAT NIGHT THE FORESTER COULD NOT SLEEP.
IF I CUT ANY MORE, THE ELEPHANT WILL SUFFER. BUT I MUST NOT BE SENTIMENTAL. I MUST GET HOLD OF THOSE PRECIOUS STUMPS OF TUSKS.
SO BACK HE WENT TO THE ELEPHANT. GREED HAD HARDENED HIS HEART.
YOUR TUSKS DID HELP TO CLEAR MY OLD DEBTS. BUT I NEED MORE MONEY IN ORDER TO LIVE.
YOU MAY HAVE WHAT IS LEFT OF MY TUSKS.
THE ELEPHANT CROUCHED DOWN TO GIVE THE TUSKS. THE MOMENT HAD COME FOR THE FORESTER TO CARRY OUT HIS CRUEL PLAN. HE PINNED THE ELEPHANT'S TRUNK DOWN WITH HIS FOOT, PULLED AT THE TUSKS...
...AND FINALLY SAWED THEM OFF.

NOW I HAVE DONE WITH YOU, MY FRIEND. I HAVE GOT ALL THERE IS TO GET.
AND HE WALKED AWAY, LEAVING THE ELEPHANT TORN AND TREMBLING. NOT A WORD OF REPROACH ESCAPED THE ELEPHANT'S LIPS.
SUDDENLY THE FORESTER FELT THE GROUND HEAVE UNDER HIS FEET. THE EARTH SPLIT OPEN AND A FIRE RAGED.
HELP! HELP!
THE FORESTER REALISED THAT HE WAS BEING PUN-ISHED FOR HIS GREED; BUT IT WAS TOO LATE.
AS THE FLAMES CONSUMED HIM, A VOICE WAS HEARD—
AN UNGRATE-FUL MAN IS NEVER SATISFIED— NOT EVEN IF HE IS GIVEN THE WHOLE WORLD.
AS FOR THE WISE ELEPHANT, HE LIVED THE REST OF HIS LIFE IN THE PEACE AND QUIET OF THE HIMALAYAS.

* BASED ON LATUKIKA JATAKA

AS THE LEADER CAME CLOSE —
O MIGHTY ELEPHANT, MY LITTLE ONES ARE IN DANGER. IF YOUR HERD ENTERS THIS GROVE, THEY WILL BE TRAMPLED TO DEATH.
DO NOT FEAR. YOUR FLEDGLINGS WILL NOT BE HARMED.
THE ELEPHANT STOOD OVER THE NEST WHILE HIS HERD GRAZED. WHEN THEY HAD HAD THEIR FILL —
THERE IS A ROGUE-ELEPHANT, A WILD AND DANGEROUS ANIMAL, WHO MIGHT SOON BE COMING THIS WAY.
WHAT SHALL I DO? I AM SO SMALL AND WEAK.
YOU MUST APPEAL TO HIM FOR MERCY AND HOPE FOR THE BEST.
SOON AFTER THE ELEPHANTS HAD GONE —
THE ROGUE-ELEPHANT!
HE LOOKS FIERCE!

THE MOTHER QUAIL WASTED NO TIME. SHE WAS AT HIS FEET, HER HEAD LOWERED IN SALUTE.
HOW DARE YOU COME IN MY WAY?
O POWERFUL ONE, I BEG OF YOU, SPARE MY YOUNG ONES!

THE ELEPHANT LASHED AT THE NEST.
THERE! THAT IS THE END OF YOUR SILLY BROOD.

AS THE QUAIL WEPT OVER THE REMAINS OF HER DEAD CHILDREN —
I WILL SOON SHOW YOU HOW STRONG I AM!

GRIEF HAD MADE HER BOLD AND SET HER THINKING HARD. SHE WENT TO A CROW AND TOLD HIM HER SAD TALE.
YOU MUST SPOT THIS ROGUE-ELEPHANT AND PECK OUT BOTH HIS EYES.
DEPEND ON ME. SUCH WICKEDNESS SHOULD NOT GO UNPUNISHED.
HAVING GOT THE CROW ON HER SIDE, THE QUAIL WENT TO AN ANT.
MY LITTLE FRIEND, I NEED YOUR HELP.
I HEARD ABOUT YOUR BABIES. I AM DEEPLY GRIEVED.
THAT IS WHY I AM HERE. WE MUST TEACH THE CRUEL ELEPHANT A LESSON.
HOW CAN I HELP?
MY FRIEND THE CROW WILL PECK OUT HIS EYES. AFTER THAT YOU MUST LAY YOUR EGGS IN THE EMPTY SOCKETS.
A GOOD IDEA! WHEN THEY HATCH, MY LITTLE ONES WILL BEGIN TO BITE.

THE QUAIL THEN WENT TO THE FROG.
DEAR FRIEND, LEAVE EVERYTHING AND COME OUT!
THE FROG ROSE TO THE SURFACE AND CROAKED.
WHAT IS THE MATTER?
ALL MY YOUNG ONES WERE CRUELLY KILLED BY A SPITEFUL ELEPHANT.
I AM TRYING TO GET MY FRIENDS TO HELP ME PUNISH HIM.
YOU CAN COUNT ON ME.
AS THEY WENT ALONG, THE QUAIL UNFOLDED HER PLANS.
••• WHEN THE ANTS HATCH, THE ROGUE-ELEPHANT WILL BE BADLY STUNG. HE WILL RUN BLINDLY, LOOKING FOR WATER TO EASE HIS PAIN. THIS IS WHAT I WANT YOU TO DO•••

A LITTLE LATER, THE CROW DARTED AT THE ELEPHANT...
...PLUCKED HIS EYES OUT. AND FLEW AWAY.
A-A-AH!
THEN, THE ANT LAID HER EGGS IN HIS BLIND EYES.
A-A-AH! MY EYES ARE ON FIRE. WATER! I NEED WATER!

JUST THEN THE FROG CROAKED FROM A STEEP PRECIPICE CLOSE BY.
CROAK
THE CROAK OF A FROG! THERE MUST BE WATER NEAR BY. I'LL FOLLOW THE SOUND.
AS THE ELEPHANT GOT TO THE EDGE OF THE PRECIPICE ...
CROAK
... THE FROG LEAPT ONTO A NARROW LEDGE BELOW AND CROAKED WITH ALL HIS MIGHT.
CROAK

THE ELEPHANT FOLLOWED THE SOUND AND WENT HURTLING DOWN TO HIS DEATH.
CRASH
WHEN THE CROW, THE ANT, THE FROG AND THE QUAIL MET LATER —
I HOPE THE STORY OF THE ELEPHANT WILL BE A GOOD EXAMPLE TO ALL STRONG CREATURES WHO HARM THE WEAK AND THE HELPLESS.

THE ROYAL ELEPHANT*

* BASED ON ALEENACHITTA JATAKA

ONE DAY, AS THEY SAT DOWN TO THEIR MIDDAY MEAL, THEY SAW AN ELEPHANT.
HE IS LIMPING AND SEEMS TO BE IN GREAT PAIN.
HE'S COMING TOWARDS US.
THE ELEPHANT CAME UP TO THE CARPENTERS AND HELD OUT A FOOT.
I STEPPED ON SOMETHING — I THINK IT'S A SPLINTER.
YOU ARE RIGHT. IT HAS ENTERED QUITE DEEP INTO THE FLESH.
THEY REMOVED THE SPLINTER, BATHED AND DRESSED THE WOUND AND NURSED THE FOOT BACK TO HEALTH.
YOU HAVE BEEN VERY KIND TO ME. I WOULD LIKE TO COME HERE EVERY DAY AND HELP YOU.
THE ELEPHANT SERVED THEM WELL FOR A NUMBER OF YEARS. ONE DAY —
LOOK! OUR FRIEND HAS BROUGHT A YOUNG ONE WITH HIM TODAY.
WHAT A BEAUTIFUL WHITE ANIMAL!

I AM NO LONGER AS ACTIVE AS I USED TO BE. I HAVE BROUGHT MY SON TO TAKE MY PLACE.
I WILL TRY MY BEST TO PLEASE YOU IN EVERY WAY.
THE YOUNG ELEPHANT WORKED HARD. HE HELPED TO LOAD AND UNLOAD TIMBER.
HE FETCHED AND CARRIED TOOLS...
...AND TRANSPORTED LOGS.
MORE, HE BROUGHT JOY AND LAUGHTER INTO THE CARPENTERS' LIVES FOR HE KEPT THEIR CHILDREN AMUSED.
OOOH! WHAT A LOVELY SWING!

ONE DAY, QUITE BY ACCIDENT, THE RAIN WASHED SOME OF HIS DROPPINGS INTO THE RIVER. LATER, DOWNSTREAM, WHERE THE ROYAL ELEPHANTS BATHED —
OUR ELEPHANTS ARE REFUSING TO GET INTO THE WATER.
LET US REPORT THE MATTER TO THE KING.
THE TRAINER GUESSED THE TRUTH.
THE WATER CONTAINS THE DROPPINGS OF A NOBLE ANIMAL. HE MUST LIVE UP-STREAM SOME-WHERE.
WHEN THE TRAINER REPORTED THE MATTER TO THE KING—
SCOUR THE COUNTRYSIDE. IF THERE IS SUCH AN ANIMAL HE SHOULD ADORN THE ROYAL STABLES.
THE KING HIMSELF SET OUT WITH A BAND OF TRUSTED MEN.
WITHIN MINUTES THEY TRACED THE ELEPHANT.
THAT MUST BE THE ANIMAL WE ARE LOOKING FOR. HOW NOBLY HE BEARS HIMSELF!

SOON —
THE KING!
DO YOU THINK HE WANTS US TO WORK IN THE PALACE?
IF HE DID, HE WOULD SEND FOR US, NOT COME HERE HIMSELF.
WHEN THE KING AND HIS PARTY DREW NEARER —
YOUR MAJESTY, WE ARE HONOURED. HOW CAN WE BE OF SERVICE TO YOU?
WE WOULD LIKE THIS ELEPHANT FOR OUR ROYAL STABLES.
THE ELEPHANT SEIZED THE OPPORTUNITY TO HELP HIS FRIENDS.
THESE MEN HAVE BEEN VERY KIND TO ME. I AM GREATLY INDEBTED TO THEM.

THE KING TURNED TO HIS MEN.
PAY THEM A HUNDRED THOUSAND PIECES OF GOLD FOR HIS TAIL, THE SAME FOR HIS TRUNK AND FOR EACH OF HIS FOUR FEET.
THE ELEPHANT WAS NOT SATISFIED.
YOU MUST NOT THINK ME GREEDY, YOUR MAJESTY. THEY NEED CLOTHES. AND THE CHILDREN TOO MUST BE PROVIDED FOR.
WE ADMIRE YOUR LOYALTY. WE SHALL MORE THAN SATISFY YOU.
UPON RECEIVING THIS ASSURANCE THE ELEPHANT AGREED TO GO WITH THE KING. IT WAS A SAD LEAVE-TAKING.
A KING'S COMMAND MUST BE OBEYED. YOU ARE GOOD CHILDREN AND WILL UNDERSTAND.
WHO WILL PLAY WITH US?
AND THE ELEPHANT LEFT FOR VARANASI WITH THE KING AND HIS MEN.

THE CITY WORE A FESTIVE AIR. THE ELEPHANT, REGALLY CAPARISONED, WAS LED TO HIS GAILY DECORATED STABLE.
THE NOBLES AND MINISTERS LOOKED ON IN ADMIRATION.
HE IS THE MOST MAJESTIC ANIMAL I HAVE EVER SEEN.
MARK MY WORDS! HE WILL PROVE HIS WORTH IN TIMES OF WAR.
THE KING MADE OVER HALF HIS KINGDOM TO THE ELEPHANT.
YOU ARE A BROTHER TO ME AND A COMPANION FOR LIFE.
THE ELEPHANT BECAME DEEPLY ATTACHED TO THE KING AND FOLLOWED HIM EVERYWHERE.
MY LORD, HE REFUSES TO TOUCH HIS FOOD TILL YOU HAVE FIRST FED HIM A MORSEL.

A FEW MONTHS LATER, THE QUEEN WAS EXPECTING A BABY.
THE ELEPHANT HAS BROUGHT US GREAT GOOD FORTUNE. MY POWER AS A MONARCH IS NOW UNCHALLENGED.
I FEEL OUR CHILD IS DESTINED FOR GREAT THINGS.
BUT THEIR JOY WAS SHORT-LIVED. THE KING FELL SERIOUSLY ILL. AS HE LAY DYING —
MY ELEPHANT WILL BE BROKEN-HEARTED.
OUR CHILD WILL NEVER KNOW A FATHER!
WHEN THE KING DIED —
WE MUST KEEP THE SAD NEWS FROM THE ELEPHANT.
I WONDER HOW LONG IT WILL BE BEFORE HE FINDS OUT!

MEANWHILE, THE KING OF KOSALA WAS MARCHING TOWARDS VARANASI.
THE KING IS DEAD, AND CONFUSION REIGNS.
THERE WERE HURRIED CONSULTATIONS AT VARANASI.
WE SHOULD ASK THEM TO SUSPEND FIGHTING FOR A WEEK.
HOW WILL THAT HELP?
ACCORDING TO THE ASTROLOGERS, THE QUEEN WILL GIVE BIRTH TO HER CHILD WITHIN A WEEK. IF IT IS A SON, WE WILL FIGHT. IF NOT, WE WILL SURRENDER.
THE KING OF KOSALA ACCEDED TO THEIR REQUEST.
A WEEK LATER —
LONG LIVE THE NEW-BORN KING!
FIGHT FOR THE KING! FIGHT TO THE LAST MAN!

THEY FOUGHT BRAVELY, BUT THE LACK OF LEADERSHIP TOLD ON THEM.
WE HAVE LOST HEAVILY.
WHAT DO YOU EXPECT? OUR LEADER LIES IN A CRADLE.
I HAVE AN IDEA. LET THE ROYAL ELEPHANT TAKE CHARGE.
THEY WENT TO THE QUEEN WHO SENT FOR THE ELEPHANT. WHILE HE GAZED AT HER SON—
HIS FATHER IS DEAD. IF THE KING MEANT ANYTHING TO YOU, HE IS NOW YOUR CHARGE.
THE KING DEAD ! WHY WAS I NOT TOLD? HOW CAN I LIVE WITH-OUT MY MASTER?
AS I DO, FOR HIS CHILD AND FOR THE KINGDOM THAT IS HIS BY RIGHT...
...AND WHICH IS AT THIS VERY MOMENT IN GRAVE DANGER.

THE ELEPHANT KNELT TO RECEIVE THE QUEEN'S BLESSING.
I SHALL TALK NO MORE OF DEATH. YOUR SON SHALL RULE.
WE NOW HAVE SOMETHING TO LIVE FOR.
AS THE KEEPER OF THE ROYAL STABLES GOT HIM READY FOR THE BATTLE...
... THE KING'S MEN FELT THEIR HOPES RISE.
GET THE TROOPS OUT! LET NO MAN DAWDLE!

AND THEN THE ELEPHANT CHARGED FORWARD, THE SKIES RESOUNDING WITH HIS MIGHTY TRUMPETING.
PUT COURAGE IN YOUR HEARTS AND STRENGTH IN YOUR ARMS!
FOLLOW OUR LEADER. HE IS DIVINELY INSPIRED!
THE KOSALA ARMIES WERE ROUTED. THE BATTLE WON, THE ELEPHANT STOOD BEFORE THE QUEEN, HIS PROUD HEAD BOWED BEFORE HIS INFANT MASTER.
MY GRIEF IS GREAT FOR YOUR DEAD FATHER. BUT I LIVE FOR YOU AND FOR THE GREAT DESTINY THAT AWAITS YOU, MY PRINCE.
AND THE BODHISATTVA (FOR THE CHILD WAS NONE OTHER THAN HE) GREW UP TO INHERIT A KINGDOM WHICH HE RULED WISELY AND WELL.

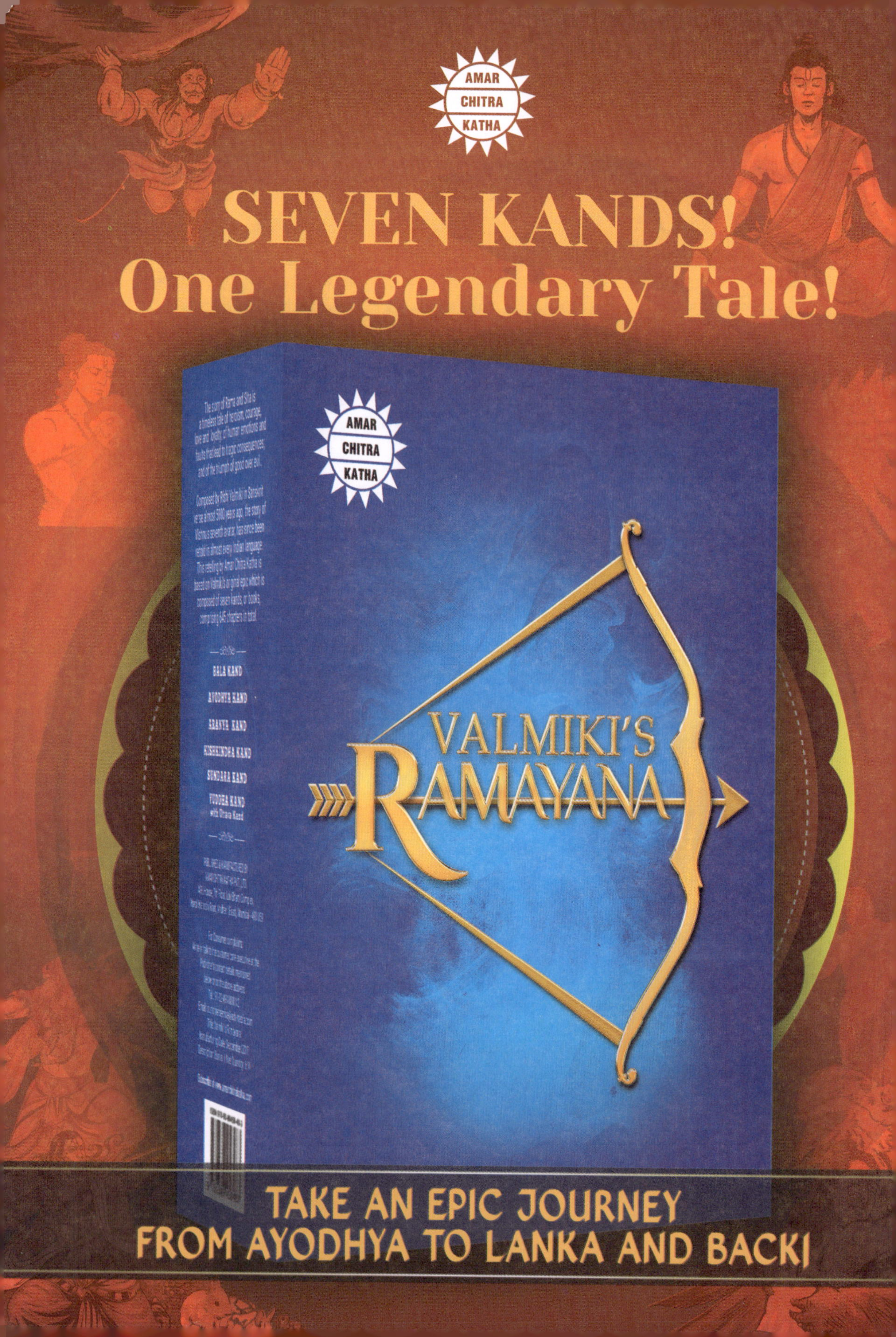
AMAR CHITRA KATHA
SEVEN KANDS!
One Legendary Tale!
AMAR CHITRA KATHA
VALMIKI'S RAMAYANA
BALA KAND
AYODHYA KAND
ARANYA KAND
KISHKINDHA KAND
SUNDARA KAND
YUDDHA KAND with Uttara Kand
TAKE AN EPIC JOURNEY
FROM AYODHYA TO LANKA AND BACK!